CONTENTS

WHAT IS PHOTOGRAPHY?

The word 'photograph' comes from the Greek word *photos*, meaning light, and *graphos*, writing. Literally, photography means 'writing with light'. The magic of photography happens when the image we saw through a camera is preserved forever on film. This book attempts to explain this magic, and the techniques everyone can use to take interesting pictures.

WRITING WITH LIGHT

No photograph is possible without light. You may have a camera, lens and film, but if there is no light source, then there will be no image to record and no photograph to create. It is the skill of the photographer in using available light which creates the best photographs.

HOW OLD IS PHOTOGRAPHY?

The first photograph was taken by the Frenchman Joseph Nicéphore Niépce in 1826. It shows the view from a window overlooking the roof of a neighbouring building. It is very shadowy, and took several hours for the picture to form. Photography as we know it today began in the 1840s, when the Englishman William Henry Fox Talbot took his early photographs at his home, Lacock Abbey, near Bath. Today, it is a museum and well worth a visit.

The advantage of Fox Talbot's system was that it enabled an infinite number of prints (positives) to be reproduced from the original image (negative). The negative/positive process is what we use in photography today.

The Frenchman, Joseph Nicéphore Niépce (left), who took the first photograph, using a bitumen-coated pewter plate. The earliest permanent photograph (below), a picture of the rooftops seen from his window, was taken in 1826 and took eight hours of exposure. He called it a *heliograph,* a drawing by the sunlight.

FOCUS ON

PHOTOGRAPHY

KEITH WILSON

HAMLYN

ACKNOWLEDGEMENTS

The publishers would like to thank the following for the loan of photographic equipment and products: Keith Johnson and Pelling Ltd, pages 11, 14-15, 22-3, 26-7, 30, 37, 38-9, 40-41, 46, 55, 66-7, 68-9; Boots the Chemist Ltd, pages 11, 37, 61, 70-71; Canon (UK) Ltd, pages 10, 36; Minolta (UK) Ltd, pages 11, 12-13; Olympus Optical Co. (UK) Ltd, page 10; the Pro Centre (Professional Equipment Hire), page 22; Olympus Sport for the sports equipment on pages 46-9; and the following individuals and organizations for permission to reproduce the pictures in this book: Allsport 47 (all pictures), 49 (all pictures). Animal Photography 52 centre left. Archiv Fur Kunst Und Geschichte 8 bottom left, 9 top left. Michael Buselle 29 bottom left, 34-5, 42 centre left, 43, 50 centre and bottom, 51 bottom right, 56 top right. Colorsport 48 top, centre and bottom. Comstock 29 top, centre left and centre right, 56 bottom right. Earthscape Editions 32 bottom left and bottom right, 33 bottom left and bottom right, 45 top left and top right. Nigel Farrow 21 (all pictures), 22 top, centre, bottom left, bottom right, 23 top right, bottom left, bottom centre, 38 top and centre, 39 top left, centre left, centre right and centre below, 46 top, 53 top. Robert Harding 61 centre right. Hulton Deutsch Collection 9 bottom left. E.A. Janes 44 (top and centre pictures). David Johnson (studio photography for Reed Children's Books): 10 top and bottom, 11 top, centre and bottom, 12-13, 13 bottom right, 14 all pictures, 15 both pictures, 18-19 background picture, 22-3 main picture, 26-7 main picture, 30 bottom, 36-7 main picture, 38 bottom right, 40 all pictures, 41 all pictures, 44-5 bottom, 45 centre, 46 bottom, 48-9 background picture, 55 bottom right, 56 bottom left, 57 all pictures, 59 main picture, 66-7 main picture, 68-9 background picture, 70-71 background picture, 74-5 main picture. Frank Lane Picture Agency 28, 33 top, 42 bottom left, 50 top, 53 right. Alan McFaden 17 all pictures, 20 both pictures, 23 bottom right, 25 both pictures, 26 top, 27 top, 39 top right and bottom, 42 top right and centre right, 52 top right, 53 centre left, 54 all pictures, 55 top left and top right, 70 top left. John Moulder 73 bottom right. NHPA 35 bottom left, 42 bottom right, 52 centre right and bottom left. Rex Features 52-3 bottom. Royal Photographic Society 9 centre right. Tony Stone Worldwide 59 top, 61 top right and bottom right, 73 top right and bottom left. Mark Summersby 73 top left. Visual Arts Library 8 bottom right. Rebecca Whitcombe 70 top right. Keith Wilson 19 all pictures except montage, 30 top left, 31 all pictures, 37 top right and bottom right, 58 all pictures, 60 bottom, 65 left, 69 right, 70 centre left, bottom left, centre right, bottom right, 72 left and bottom right, 75 centre.

Illustrators:
David Ashby (Garden Studio): 12, 15, 16, 61,65, 66, 68, 69, 71. Peter Bull Art: 24, 34, 36, 38, 51, 55.

20 00004 426

Editors: Andrew Farrow, Julie West, Bobbi Whitcombe
Designers: Anne Sharples, Mark Summersby
Series Designer: Anne Sharples
Production Controller: Linda Spillane
Picture Researcher: Anna Smith

Published in 1994 by
Hamlyn Children's Books,
an imprint of Reed Children's Books,
Michelin House, 81 Fulham Road,
London SW3 6RB,
and Auckland, Melbourne,
Singapore and Toronto.

ISBN 0 600 57473 3

Printed in Great Britain

WHAT IS PHOTOGRAPHY?

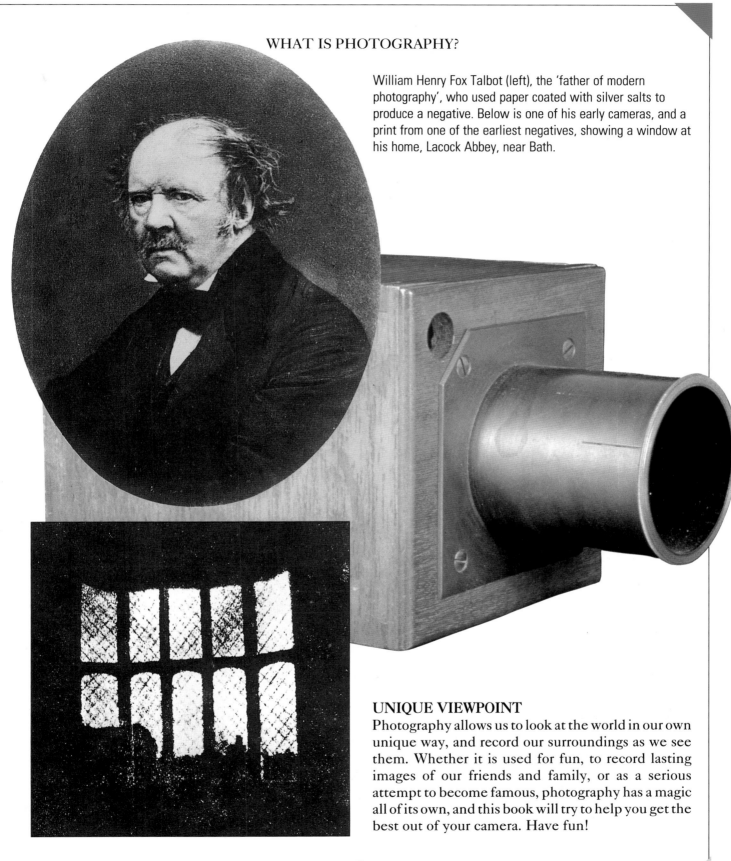

William Henry Fox Talbot (left), the 'father of modern photography', who used paper coated with silver salts to produce a negative. Below is one of his early cameras, and a print from one of the earliest negatives, showing a window at his home, Lacock Abbey, near Bath.

UNIQUE VIEWPOINT

Photography allows us to look at the world in our own unique way, and record our surroundings as we see them. Whether it is used for fun, to record lasting images of our friends and family, or as a serious attempt to become famous, photography has a magic all of its own, and this book will try to help you get the best out of your camera. Have fun!

There are hundreds of different cameras on the market of all shapes, sizes, prices and specification. This may seem a little daunting at first. However, remember that a camera is an expensive item, so think carefully about what you want to get out of your photography. You should be able to find one to suit you. The adverts and articles in photo magazines can be helpful, by giving recommendations and costs.

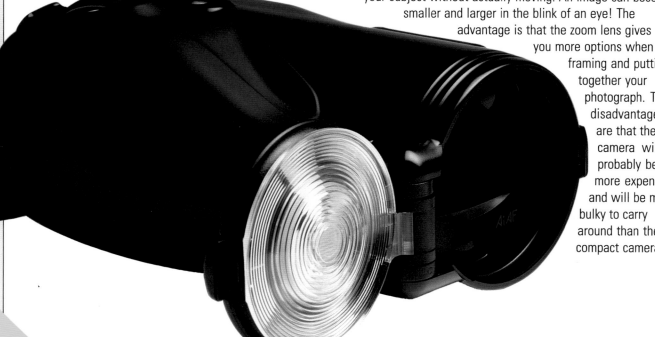

COMPACT CAMERAS

These (above right) are cameras which are small enough to fit in your pocket. Focusing, exposure and film advance are usually done automatically, so all you have to do is look through the camera and press the shutter when you want to take your picture. Many also have a built-in flash, making indoor photography as easy as outdoor. The quality of photos from this type of camera is usually good.

ZOOM CAMERAS

The first camera with a built-in zoom lens was made in 1986. Since then, zoom cameras have become increasingly popular. This type of camera allows you to get closer to your subject without actually moving. An image can become smaller and larger in the blink of an eye! The advantage is that the zoom lens gives you more options when framing and putting together your photograph. The disadvantages are that the camera will probably be more expensive, and will be more bulky to carry around than the compact camera.

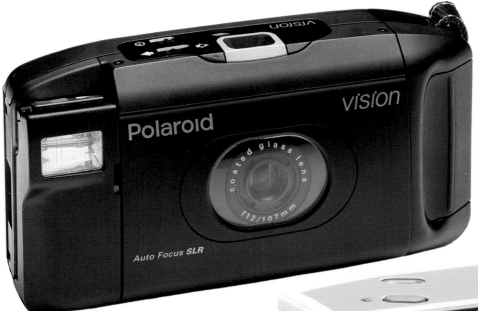

INSTANT CAMERAS

Polaroid cameras are unique for their ability to produce a colour print which develops in front of your eyes in just a few minutes. The first Polaroid camera was made by Edwin Land in 1947, when he took up the challenge of his three-year-old daughter to see a photo immediately after it had been taken. Polaroid cameras are low priced and use their own special film to make the instant picture.

DISPOSABLE CAMERAS

These are among the cheapest cameras you can buy, but can only be used for one roll of film. (The camera is recycled by the processors.) They are made by Kodak, Agfa, Konica and Fuji, and are sold already loaded with colour print film. There are different types of disposable cameras: flash versions, as well as panorama and underwater models.

SLR (SINGLE LENS REFLEX) CAMERAS

Professionals and press photographers, as well as keen amateur photographers, use SLRs. The main advantage of an SLR camera is that there is a wide range of interchangeable lenses to choose from. SLR camera lenses are better quality than zoom camera lenses. The other advantage is that an SLR gives you exactly the same view through the viewfinder as the lens. While bigger than compacts, SLRs are much lighter than they used to be. The latest models include many of the automatic features found on a compact or zoom camera, as well as manual controls.

HOW AN SLR CAMERA WORKS

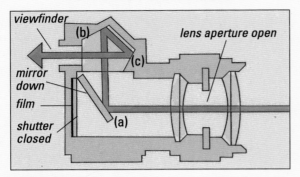

When you look through the viewfinder, the reflex mirror is down, so the light coming through the lens is reflected by three separate surfaces (a, b, and c) into your eye. You see the exact image that will fall on the film.

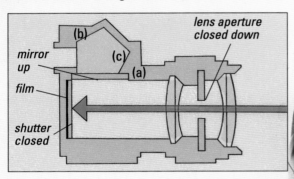

When you press the shutter release button, the mirror (a) moves up out of the way, and the lens aperture (see page 24) closes down to allow just the right amount of light into the camera.

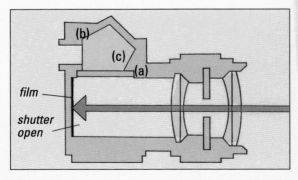

When this has happened, the shutter opens and the light from the image hits the film at the back of the camera.

WHAT IS AN SLR?

SLR stands for single lens reflex. Looking through the viewfinder of an SLR camera, the image you see is the one you will eventually see on your photograph. Light bounces off three reflective surfaces between the lens and your eye. When you press the shutter button, the mirror in front of the film will rise out of the way, blocking the viewfinder, and the shutter blind will open to allow the light from your subject to hit the film in your camera. Once this has happened, the photo is recorded on your film. The mirror will then swing down again, and you will be able to see the original image again through the viewfinder.

THINGS TO CONSIDER WHEN YOU BUY A CAMERA

Size and weight. You should choose a camera that will be comfortable in your hands and not too heavy to hold, especially if you plan on being out and about for long periods of time.

Ease of use. Many cameras are totally automated so all you have to do is point and shoot. But if you want a camera that enables you to focus the lens or decide when to use flash, make sure these controls are easy to use.

Lens quality. The lens determines the quantity and quality of light that will reach the film. Many cameras look the same, but their results could be very different because the lens of one is much better than the others.

Subject choice. The type of pictures you take should influence the camera you choose. For example, if you like taking pictures by the sea, look for a camera that is going to be water and sand resistant. If you want to take photos of flowers or insects, make sure your camera can focus at close range.

Accessories. The way certain cameras are designed means that you can add accessories to them as you learn more about photography. This is especially true of SLR cameras.

Lenses. When buying an SLR, remember that certain lenses will not fit on to certain cameras. This means that Minolta lenses will not fit a Canon camera; Nikon lenses will not fit a Pentax, etc. However, independent lens makers such as Sigma, Tamron and Tokina make lenses to fit most brands of SLR.

'hot shoe' for optional flash gun

lock/on switch

self timer

zooming ring

lens

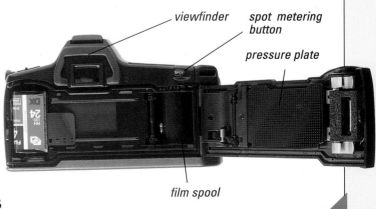

viewfinder

spot metering button

pressure plate

film spool

LOADING AND HOLDING

Loading modern cameras is easy. With practice, it should become second nature to you, so that you can load your camera very quickly, and not miss any exciting shots because you have forgotten what to do!

Try taking your photographs from all sorts of different angles and positions. Just make sure you're steady and feel comfortable before you squeeze the shutter button.

HOW TO HOLD YOUR CAMERA

Hold the camera firmly in both hands, but not too tight. When holding the camera to your eye, keep your arms close to your body by tucking your elbows to your sides. Make sure your fingers aren't creeping over the lens. If your camera has a built-in flash, make sure your fingers aren't obscuring any part of the flash.

Breathe gently and slowly. When you're ready to take your photograph, hold your breath, but don't take a deep breath. Squeeze the shutter button gently down. Breathe out.

RECOGNIZING CAMERA SHAKE

It is important to hold your camera properly. Most blurred, fuzzy photographs are caused by camera shake. If you jerk your camera or tremble while pressing the shutter button, you will get a photo that will look soft and unsharp. Using a camera that is too heavy for you will cause camera shake. Trying to take a picture while the light is too low will also show up any movement you make while holding the camera.

HOW TO LOAD YOUR CAMERA

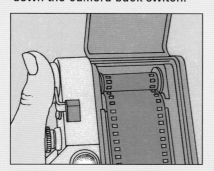

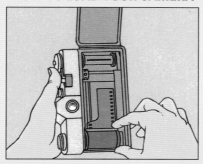

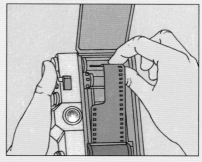

1. Make sure you've rewound the old film. Then, open the back by pulling up the rewind knob or sliding down the camera back switch.

2. Put a cassette in the film chamber. Make sure the leader is on the outside, then gently pull it across the camera back to the take-up spool.

3. Insert the film leader into the slit of the take-up spool, making sure the bottom line of sprocket holes is over the sprocket.

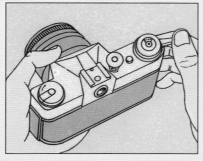

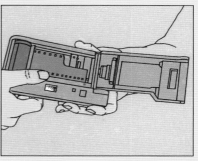

4. Wind on the film by pressing the shutter release button and moving the wind-on lever. Repeat until top and bottom sprocket holes engage.

5. Close the camera back and continue winding on until the first frame (1) appears in the frame counter window.

6. Automatics: After 2, pull the film leader across to the mark on the spool chamber, then close it. A motor will wind the film on.

It is helpful to rest your arms on a wall or ledge, or press them firmly in to your sides, to keep the camera steady.

USING A CAMERA

The more you use a camera the more familiar you will become with how it works. Your confidence will grow, too, and your pictures will improve. You should read the instruction book for a new camera, and play around with the camera, before loading it with film. Get used to how it feels, familiarize yourself with the controls and how they operate, and learn what the viewfinder information and LED (light emitting diode) symbols all mean.

Use your first few films to see what the camera can do, and take notes of what you did, the weather conditions, and what controls were used for each picture. Then, when you look at your first set of photographs, or prints, you can see the result and, by referring to your notes, know why the picture looked the way it did. Above all, be patient. Taking good photographs requires practice and time.

FOCUSING
Nearly all cameras made today use auto focus. This works by aiming the focusing frame in the centre of your camera's viewfinder at the subject you want in focus. With an SLR, as soon as you aim the focusing frame at your subject, you can see it coming into focus. This is confirmed for you by a shining green LED light which appears in the viewfinder.

FOCUS LOCK
Try this trick with an SLR camera to make your photos look a bit different. If you want to keep the subject in focus, but recompose the picture so the subject is off centre, then gently squeeze the shutter button halfway down. This is called focus lock and enables you to move the focusing frame off your subject, without it going out of focus. When you have your picture composed the way you want, complete the press of the shutter button to take your picture. Remember, lifting your finger from the half-press position will undo the focus lock.

MANUAL FOCUS
SLRs allow you to focus automatically (letting the camera take control) or manually (with you in the driving seat). The focusing frame of a manual focus SLR is called a split screen.

When you point your camera at the part of the scene you want in focus, look for a distinct line to focus on. If the scene is out of focus, the split screen in the central focusing frame will show any lines as broken or unaligned.

As you turn the lens focusing ring, you will see these broken lines within the split screen come together. When the lines join up, that part of the scene is focused. Concentrate on something vertical, such as a tree, and watch as its shape moves out of line then comes into focus right in front of your eyes!

The SLR viewfinder has a split screen which joins up as you adjust the focus. When the lines come together, the scene is in focus.

EXPOSURE

Exposure means the amount of light which falls on the film when you press the shutter button. This is controlled by the shutter speed (the length of time the shutter is left open) and the size of the aperture (the hole in the lens diaphragm: see page 24). On a bright, sunny day you will need a small aperture to limit the amount of light that enters the camera. In dull weather, or darker conditions, you need to use a wider aperture. The shutter speed is also affected by the amount of light available. With a darker scene, using a slow shutter speed will help you to get a sharper image. If there is movement in your picture, however, too slow a shutter speed will give a blurred image.

Sometimes, a camera can let too much light on to the film, and the picture, like the one above, will look washed-out and lack contrast. This is called over-exposure.

If there is not enough light on the film, the picture will look dark and lack detail (like the one on the right). This is called under-exposure.

With the correct aperture and shutter speed, your picture should be bright and clear, with plenty of detail. This picture shows the buildings clearly, as well as the cloud patterns and the reflected sunset colours on the water, without appearing either too pale or too dark.

Many of today's cameras can set the exposure automatically. This setting is called Program and it is found on all compact cameras, zoom cameras and most SLRs. In even lighting conditions it gives you correct exposures every time. This means you can be ready to shoot at any time, without worrying that the picture will not be exposed correctly. You can then spend your time concentrating on the scene in front of you, not on the controls of your camera.

However, when you are more experienced, you may want a camera on which you can control the exposure yourself, and experiment with various techniques.

GETTING STARTED

No matter what camera you are using, there are some things about taking photographs which apply to all. There are some very basic points to remember so that you avoid problems at the start. Your motto should be LOOK BEFORE YOU SHOOT!

Before pressing the shutter button check the following:
1. You have film in your camera.
2. Everything you want in the picture is inside the frame edge marks of the viewfinder.
3. The sun is not shining directly into the lens - this will cause 'flare' and fool your camera into under-exposing.
4. Your fingers are clear of the lens and flash.
5. The camera is in focus - a green light in the viewfinder will confirm this on an SLR.

You will find plenty of occasions to take photographs once you've got a camera: be prepared to experiment with people, places, pets, indoors and outdoors.

PRACTICE SHOTS

You have one roll of 24 exposure colour print film loaded into your new camera. It's your first roll, but what will you shoot? Here are some suggestions:

Take a picture of your mum and dad outside. You could take one shot with the camera in its usual horizontal position, and one vertically.

Now take a picture of them inside; first with flash, then without flash but with the house lights on instead.

Take a group shot of the whole family outside, some sitting, others standing, and check all corners of the frame to make sure everyone's in.

Switch the TV on and take a picture of it without flash. Try different shutter speeds - what difference do they make to the picture?

Take a picture of yourself in front of the mirror, remembering to focus on the reflection - not on the surface of the glass.

Take a picture of the view through your bedroom window. If you can't open the window, rest the lens against the glass. This will keep any reflection to a minimum.

Shoot the sunset. Alternatively, mount the camera on a tripod and, using a telephoto lens, shoot the moon. No flash required.

A NEW ANGLE

When you see something you want to photograph, try different angles to see which would make the most interesting picture. Crouch down with your camera, or look at the scene from a different direction. If your camera has a zoom lens, try zooming closer for a different view. Try holding it vertically - people and tall buildings often look better from this angle.

Shot from a medium distance, this collection of buildings makes an interesting urban landscape, with the colourful murals and contrasting shapes. But from immediately below the tall building, looking up, you get a quite different effect, with the pattern of lines emphasising height and distance.

MEASURING LIGHT
Many SLR cameras have more than one system, or exposure mode, for measuring light.

Spot/Partial. Takes a light reading from a small area in the centre of the frame. Ideal for photos of people, close-ups or subjects illuminated among shadows, like these ponies.

Centre weighted. Measures light from the whole frame area but gives an average value weighted towards the centre and lower half of the frame. Good for landscapes.

Evaluative/Multi-pattern. Divides the frame into a number of separate areas and measures light from each, then computes an average. Excellent in scenes of high contrast.

TIPS AND HINTS

Photography is about using the light and lens of your camera to create a picture that will reflect what you see. Because cameras today can focus and expose automatically, it is very easy to take a picture quickly. But don't take it too quickly. Make sure everything in the viewfinder is exactly as you want it, then fire.

If you are shooting outdoors, watch how the light changes during the course of the day. It is wise to keep the sun behind you, but when taking photos of people outdoors try to keep the sun out of their eyes. If you don't they will squint, and this will spoil the look of the picture.

DISTRACTION

Before taking your picture, check to make sure there are no distracting objects or colours either in front of, or behind, the subject. For instance, a portrait of a friend could be spoiled if a large red bus looms up right behind her head! You may only need to move your subject a few feet to left or right to overcome the problem, as you can see in the pictures on the right.

To get a good, well-balanced shot, you should think ahead - is the most important part of the picture a person, an object, a colour, or movement? Concentrate on this central idea, and then focus directly on it to get the best picture possible.

In the first photograph (left), the boy is squinting because of the bright sunlight, and the shadows produce a harsh contrast. In the second, the sunlight is diffused, so we see more detail - and a happier smile!

HIGHLIGHT AND SHADOW

It is important to be aware of the amount of contrast in a scene when looking through your camera's viewfinder. Contrast is the measure of difference between bright areas (highlights) and dark areas (shadows).

Remember that the brighter the sun, the darker the shadows, so contrast will be high. This can cause problems for your camera's light meter.

For example, if your subject is in shadow and the background is brightly lit, the camera will be tricked into making a proper exposure for the bright background and thereby make your friend - the subject of your picture - appear dark: in silhouette.

The answer is always to expose for your subject, press the shutter button halfway to lock the exposure, recompose, then press all the way to take the picture. Cameras with built-in spot metering systems make exposing for your subject even more accurate when used in this way.

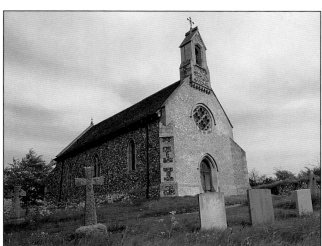

In the top photograph, the high proportion of sky has caused the camera to under-expose, so the church is almost silhouetted. With the exposure adjusted (below), the building is clearer and the whole picture is brighter.

PHOTO HINT
Always protect your camera and equipment, and keep it clean. Invest in a good storage case or bag, and remember to put everything away safely after use.

LENSES

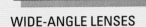

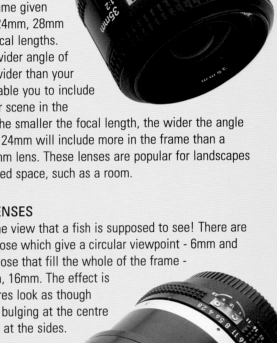

The lens is the eye of the camera. Like your own eyes it should be kept clean at all times to give best results. Your eyes give you the same angle of view all the time, like the fixed lens of a compact camera. But SLR cameras can change the way you see things because you can change lenses. Imagine what it would be like if your own eye could move closer to a subject, but without you physically moving yourself, - as a zoom lens does! There are dozens of different types of lenses which you can use with an SLR camera. Each is designed for a purpose, and some are more specialist than others.

WIDE-ANGLE LENSES

This is the name given to lenses of 24mm, 28mm and 35mm focal lengths. They give a wider angle of view, much wider than your eyes, and enable you to include a much larger scene in the viewfinder. The smaller the focal length, the wider the angle of view, so a 24mm will include more in the frame than a 28mm or 35mm lens. These lenses are popular for landscapes or in a confined space, such as a room.

FISH-EYE LENSES

These give the view that a fish is supposed to see! There are two types, those which give a circular viewpoint - 6mm and 8mm - and those that fill the whole of the frame - 14mm, 15mm, 16mm. The effect is weird - pictures look as though everything is bulging at the centre and falling in at the sides.

STANDARD LENS

Until recently all SLR cameras were sold with a lens of 50mm focal length (see page 24), known as a standard lens - because the field of view is similar to the human eye.

PORTRAIT LENSES

Also called short telephoto lenses, these are thought to be the best for portrait photography because they don't distort the image in any way. They range from 85mm to 105mm in focal length and let in a lot of light.

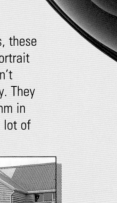

TELEPHOTO LENSES

These are the big ones. They give a small angle of view but allow you to get a close look at your subject, even though you may be a long distance from it. Sports and wildlife photographers use telephoto lenses all the time. Focal lengths are: 135mm, 180mm, 200mm, 300mm, 400mm, 600mm and 800mm. The longer the focal length, the bigger the lens and the closer the view.

ZOOM LENSES

The most popular of all because they include many focal lengths in one lens, saving you time changing lenses, as well as space. Although these lenses tend to be more expensive than individual fixed focus lenses, they will cost you less than buying the whole set! They come in all lengths and sizes: wide-angle (21-35mm, 24-50mm); standard (28-70mm, 35-70mm, 35-105mm); and telephoto (70-210mm, 80-200mm, 75-300mm).

MACRO LENSES

Specially designed for close-up photography, these lenses can focus extremely close and give a half life-size or full life-size image of small flowers and insects.

WHAT IS FOCAL LENGTH?

Focal length is the distance from the centre of the lens to the point at which the image of a distant object is in sharp focus. The longer the focal length, the narrower the angle of view, and the bigger the image. Wide-angle lenses have a short focal length; telephoto lenses a long focal length.

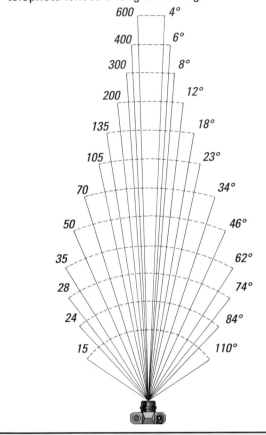

600	4°
400	6°
300	8°
200	12°
135	18°
105	23°
70	34°
50	46°
35	62°
28	74°
24	84°
15	110°

WHAT'S IN A LENS?

A camera lens contains more than one piece of glass. Each piece is called an element and is very pure, clear and well polished. Zoom lenses contain more elements than fixed focal lengths - as many as 13 or 14 pieces! Some elements are paired very closely to each other. Such a pairing is called a group. The rear of the lens contains the mount which locks on to the throat of the camera. The front lens element can vary considerably in size from lens to lens. Large telephoto lenses use big front lens elements to gather in more light, thus increasing the lens's maximum aperture. These are called fast lenses.

WHAT IS DEPTH OF FIELD?

Depth of field is the term given to the depth of a picture that is in focus. It is controlled largely by the lens aperture and also the focal length of the lens. For instance, long focal length lenses such as telephotos have a narrow depth of field, so focusing has to be precise for your subject to be in focus. Wide-angle lenses, by contrast, have a very large depth of field, so most of your picture area will look sharp. Depth of field increases as you decrease the size of the lens aperture, so an aperture of f/16 will give much more depth of field than f/4.

In these two pictures, the first one (right), taken at an aperture of f/1.4, shows the railings in the centre in focus, but the leaves and the rest of the railings are out of focus. The second photograph (far right), taken at f/22, shows the whole scene sharply in focus.

WHAT IS AN F NUMBER?

Most cameras control the amount of light passing through the lens by adjusting the size of the hole (aperture) in the lens diaphragm. The settings which adjust this are called f numbers. A typical average range of f numbers would be f/2 (a wide aperture - letting in the most light), through f/2.8, f/4, f/5.6, f/8, f/11 down to f/16 (a small aperture - letting in the least light). As you move down this range , each 'stop' lets in half as much light as before. For instance, an aperture of f/4 lets in half as much as an aperture of f/2.8, but twice as much light as an aperture of f/5.6.

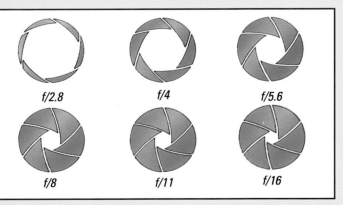

f/2.8   f/4   f/5.6

f/8   f/11   f/16

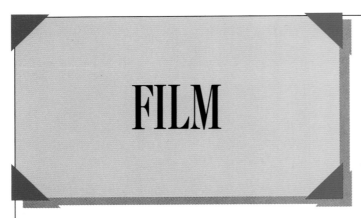

FILM

Film is used to capture your image permanently. Film holds all the light reflected off the subject you photograph, and produces an image when developed. It is a strip of transparent plastic, coated with chemicals which are extremely sensitive to light, and only takes an instant to be exposed correctly.

Not all film is the same. The most popular is colour negative, and the oldest existing film type is black and white negative. Most colour films are daylight balanced, which means they are made to accurately reflect colours lit by sunlight.

EXPOSURE LENGTHS

Films are sold in 12, 24 and 36 frame lengths. For trying out your camera, or for a small number of pictures of a particular subject, your pet for example, the 12 exposure film is probably best. For holidays or action photos needing continuous shooting action, such as a race, the longer lengths are ideal.

FILM SPEED

Every film has a speed known as an ISO (International Standards Organization) number, which is a measure of the film's sensitivity to light. A film with an ISO of 400 is twice as sensitive to light as an ISO 200 film, which is twice as sensitive as an ISO 100 film. In very bright sunlight, where there is a lot of reflection from water or

Film can be bought in a range of speeds and with a variety of numbers of frames or exposures. Remember, the faster the film, the grainier it will be if you enlarge it.

look for expiry/'use by' date on reverse of box

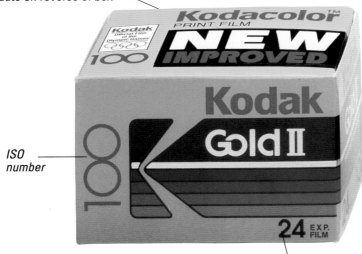

ISO number

number of frames

26

snow, it is best to use a slow film speed. In poor light, indoors, or using flash, it is best to use a faster film speed such as ISO 400. It is important to remember that the faster the film speed, the grainier the photograph (like the photo on the right below). Although this won't be so noticeable on normal size prints, it will if the print is enlarged.

SLIDES

Unlike colour negative, the cost of colour slide film usually includes processing. Slide film isn't developed the same way as colour negative, because it produces a positive image on the film itself. There are no negatives, as the slides you get are actually your film, and they will be mounted in cardboard or plastic frames for easy viewing.

SLIDES OR PRINTS

A good reason for choosing colour negative (which gives you prints) rather than colour slide film is that it tends to correct over- and under-exposure. With colour slide film, your exposures have to be spot on. However, when it comes to the quality of colour, slide film is much sharper and the colours do not fade as quickly.

COMPOSITION

Composition has very few tools - your eye and the viewfinder of the camera - but an infinite number of possibilities. It is your eye, and how you see the world, which makes your pictures unique. How you put together your photograph depends on which elements strike you as interesting and useful for your picture. Understanding these influences and the way they attract your eye can help you achieve well-composed photographs every time.

FOCAL POINT

Most good pictures have a focal point - that part of a photograph which is the main area of interest. It is the area that the eye is drawn to, and is usually the reason for taking the photograph. It can be any shape or size, and contain any number of elements. The important thing is to arrange the picture area so that the focal point always remains the most important element of your picture.

Notice how the eye is drawn towards the stag by the contrast of dark and light colours, the way the light colour narrows towards it, and the way the out-of-focus foreground leads you towards the sharper main image.

28

WHAT TO LOOK FOR

Colour. Colours help to define the shape and form of subjects. However, some colours can dominate a composition on their own by adding emphasis to a focal point. For instance, red is a very dominant colour and stands out from practically any scene.

Lines. Whether they are natural or man-made, lines are everywhere - the horizon, a flight of steps, a road or footpath, an avenue of trees, a river bend. Lines lead the eye within the picture and can be used to direct the viewer to a focal point.

Shapes. Look out for interesting shapes in the triangles formed by roofs, the rectangles of doors and windows, the curves of a bowl of fruit - or even a group of people .

Position and balance. Scenes of more than one subject area will lead your eye from one focal point to the other. How you position these subjects can dramatically alter the balance of the picture. For instance, two objects of the same size next to each other will give an even, well-balanced photo. If one of them is behind, and you focus on the nearer one, you'll have an imbalanced but probably more forceful composition .

WHAT IS THE RULE OF THIRDS?

When taking a photo, try to divide your picture space into thirds, both horizontally and vertically. The points where the lines cross mark the strongest areas for your composition. Placing your subject in the centre of the frame can make a very static picture. However, if it is positioned on one of these points, it makes the whole photo come alive! The horizon should either be aligned in the top third of the frame or the bottom, but never across the centre. Try out some pictures yourself and see what different results you can achieve by following this simple guide.

You can alter the composition of a photograph by using an adjustable framer on a print to select and then enlarge part of it.

CHECKPOINTS

When you have seen something you want to photograph, consider the following before you press the shutter button:

Are you close enough? You might be able to improve the composition by moving a few steps closer.

Does your subject have a distinctive shape or colour? If so, this could form the focal point of your picture if it stands out from the rest of the scene.

Are there any obvious 'leading lines'? Look for any roads and paths which will help lead your eye into the photo.

Is the background clear and unobtrusive? A cluttered background will distract the eye from the subject. A clear, neutral background will help emphasize the position, shape and substance of your subject.

How have you framed the scene? The viewfinder is the picture frame, and its edges are the most important lines of all, determining the size, scale, position and balance of all that lies within.

CHANGING YOUR COMPOSITION

A zoom lens is a great aid to changing the composition of your picture. As you zoom in and out, see how your subjects change in size, shape and importance. Your focal point may alter as other features enter the frame or grow in size.

Whereas the main photograph captures a wide, varied cityscape, zooming in on the bridge, the boats or the river with St Paul's as a feature will enable you to highlight different aspects of the same picture.

USING LIGHT

A good photographer will be able to use the changing qualities of light to achieve dynamic results. The sun is the greatest light source of all. It gives colour to everything, and during the course of a day those colours can change dramatically.

THE COLOUR OF LIGHT

When the sun is overhead, the sky is blue, but at sunrise and sunset we all marvel at the golden orange colour of the sky. The difference in colour is due to the way light is scattered through the atmosphere during the course of the day. Light is made up of all colours of the spectrum ranging from ultra violet (UV) to infra red (IR). UV has a short wavelength and is more easily scattered, so it is only on a clear day with the sun high in the sky that the sky will appear blue. At the lower angle of sunrise and sunset, the sun's rays pass through more atmosphere, scattering the blue UV light and leaving the longer-waved IR light to colour the sky red.

Changes in the light at different times of day can make a remarkable difference to a scene, as is obvious from these four photographs taken in the early morning...

THE NATURE OF LIGHT

To understand the nature of light consider how a fixed part of the landscape, such as the house and garden in the four photographs below, alters in appearance as the position and intensity of the sun changes.

When the sun rises in the east, the house will be lit by a warm colour, which brings out the golden tones of the wooden door. Many of the trees still look dark. Long shadows will be cast to the west, away from us, but they are toned down by the softer early morning light, and the colours are muted.

As the sun climbs higher, the shadows shorten, and the light is at its brightest and most harsh. The difference between areas of highlight and shadow - contrast - becomes much greater. The rich green colour of the trees and grass are emphasized, and the brilliant tones of the flowers and the blue of the sky now become intense.

As the sun begins its afternoon dip to the west, it has become slightly overcast; the contrast is much reduced and the light is more even. Shadows and colours are again toned down.

At sunset, the golden tones of the setting sun just catch some of the leaves of the tree on the left. The light is fading rapidly, giving the garden the dusky atmosphere of early evening - while one last glancing ray of sunlight has caught and been reflected in the lens of the camera, to give a mini-rainbow.

mid-morning...

ATMOSPHERE

The presence of mist, fog or cloud can dramatically affect the quality of light. Early morning mist or fog can be an important element in a picture, particularly when photographing landscapes. It can soften the light and reduce subject detail and contrast, giving a soft, dreamy effect.

Clouds can filter or reflect the rays of the sun, depending on their thickness and the sun's position. When there is a lot of cloud cover during the day, shadows tend to disappear, and there is less contrast between objects. Therefore, the light is more even. A spectacular result can be achieved when there are a lot of clouds at sunset. Try taking a picture from the same place at different times of day to see atmosphere in action!

late afternoon...

and at sunset.

TYPES OF LIGHTING

Frontal. This is light, either natural or artificial, which shines from behind the camera directly on to the subject being photographed.

Edge. Also known as side-lighting, this is usually a single light source which is directed from the side of the camera to emphasize subject shape and texture.

Back lighting. The light source shines towards the camera lens illuminating the subject from behind. This creates a silhouette with very little colour.

Mixed lighting. This is when two or more different light sources, such as daylight or tungsten electric lamps, combined with flash from the camera, are used to photograph a subject.

You don't have to have a sunny summer's day to get an interesting photograph. You can get some fascinating results from poor weather conditions, using the contrasts between dark and light that changes in the weather can produce. Notice how the rainbow (left) shows up against the gloomy sky, and the contrast is repeated in the rows of vines below it. The sunlight on a shaded pond (below) has brought out the warm colours of the reflections. The low angle of the sun on the snow (below right) makes interesting bluish shadows on the track, which increase the feeling of cold.

LIGHT AND FILM

Although the human eye does not make a distinction between daylight and other forms of light, film registers their true colours. For example, household lamps are tungsten, and when exposed to film give a pleasing, warm orange cast. Fluorescent lights give a strong green cast when photographed.

Most film is daylight balanced, meaning it is made to accurately record the colours of scenes lit by sunlight. Tungsten films compensate for the orange cast of a light bulb to make the scene appear as if it has been lit by daylight.

WEATHER EFFECTS

A change in the weather can often produce a stunning result when photographed. Watch how the effect of light changes with the weather. After a rainstorm, try to capture the sudden effect of sunlight on water, reflections in a puddle, a rainbow in the sky, or a bright collection of umbrellas as people battle home through the rain. Other weather effects can be equally dramatic: the transformation of objects after it has snowed, the rage of a thunderstorm and the heat haze when the weather is hot!

FLASH PHOTOGRAPHY

The addition of flash to your camera provides an extra light source which you can use and control, increasing the number and type of photos you can take. A lot of people think flash should only be used indoors or at night, but it is more versatile than that.

FILL-IN FLASH

In backlit scenes where the foreground is cast in shadow and image detail is lost, flash can add the necessary frontal lighting to fill in the shadows and illuminate detail. If you're photographing someone with the sun behind you, it means the sun will be shining into their eyes, causing them to squint. This is uncomfortable and not very flattering. The answer is to swap positions so that your model has the sun behind them and is subsequently backlit. You then take your picture using flash to supply the frontal lighting.

WHAT IS A GUIDE NUMBER?

A guide number (GN) is a measure of a flashgun's power. The larger the GN, the more powerful the flash. Guide numbers are usually measured in metres or feet and quoted for ISO 100 speed film.

Dividing the guide number by the camera-to-subject distance will give you the aperture needed for an accurate flash exposure. For example, using a flashgun with GN20 on a subject five feet away will require an aperture of f/4.

Some flash units fit on top of the camera, attached by the 'hot shoe'. There are also flash units which are built into the camera, and are totally automatic. When switched on they instantly set the shutter to the flash sync speed. This ensures almost flawless flash exposures every time. Remember that separate units require batteries, which need changing regularly.

DIRECTING FLASH

The one drawback about flash is that it is a very harsh directional source of light and can cast dark outlines of shadow. Some flash units which fit on to a camera's hot shoe have adjustable heads which allow you to bounce the flash off a white wall or ceiling. This reduces the intensity of the flash and scatters the light evenly across a wider area (diffusion).

automatic flash

FLASH SYNCHRONIZATION

Every camera has a flash synchronization (sync) speed which is the fastest shutter speed that should be used with your camera's flash. Common flash sync speeds are 1/60sec, 1/100sec, 1/125sec and 1/250sec.

Some SLR cameras allow you to set shutter speeds. If you select a faster shutter speed than the flash sync speed, your pictures will have dark bands across them with no image detail. These bands are the camera's shutter blinds passing across the film while the flash was on. It is all right to use a slower shutter speed than the flash sync speed, as this will allow any other light sources to be picked up as well as the detail lit by the flash burst.

THE CURSE OF RED-EYE!

Flash pictures which turn the pupils of your subject's eyes blood-red are the most unflattering photos of all. Red-eye is caused by the flash illuminating the blood vessels at the back of the eye at the moment of exposure. The lens will reflect this onto film if the flash is too close to it - often the case with cameras featuring built-in flash units. However, many modern cameras now feature 'red-eye reduction systems', most of which fire a pre-flash to contract the eye's pupil before firing the main flash exposure! This reduces the effect.

A clear case of red-eye: notice the wide pupils.

Red-eye reduction: the pupils have contracted.

separate flash unit

'hot shoe'

automatic flash

FILTERS

Natural light is known as white light, but it is actually made up of all the colours of the spectrum. Filters are designed to be attached to the lens of your camera either to block some of these colours entering your lens or to change the way the light falls on to the film.

SKYLIGHT AND UV FILTERS
These are the most common filters. Both eliminate ultra violet light and haze, but neither radically alters a scene's appearance, so many photographers use them to protect their lenses from dust, grit and moisture.

FILTER FACTORS
Because some filters block some of the light passing through the lens, you could end up under-exposing your picture. To avoid this, take an exposure reading of the scene without the filter and then increase your exposure with the filter on the lens by the maker's recommended 'filter factor' written on the box.

HOW DO FILTERS WORK?

Coloured or graduated filters block all but one colour of light from passing through your lens. For example, a red filter will only let red light through the lens, thereby turning everything red. On black and white film a red filter will darken a scene, especially skies. Other filters such as starbursts, multi-image and polarising filters cause the light to diffract and scatter to produce specific effects.

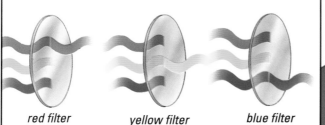

red filter   *yellow filter*   *blue filter*

GRADUATED FILTERS
Clearly recognizable by a coloured top half and clear lower half, graduated filters are mostly used to add bold colour to an otherwise uninteresting-looking sky. The area of gradation from colour to clear is very

No filter

Red graduated filter

narrow, so you should use a large aperture, say f/4 or f/5.6, to make a seamless join between the two halves. Popular colours for these filters are red, orange, blue, yellow and tobacco.

Tobacco graduated filter

Blue graduated filter

POLARISING FILTERS

Natural light vibrates in all directions, the waves travelling in all sorts of planes. When reflected off a non-metal surface, light becomes polarised: it travels in a single plane. A polarising filter will only let the limited polarised light vibrations pass through it. It is particularly useful for reducing reflections off glass or water, giving you a clearer view of people inside a glass-fronted building, or fish below the water's surface.

A polarising filter has a rotating mount. When you turn it, you can see how things change. It can make the sky look darker and bluer, but best results are achieved when the lens is pointed 90° to the sun's position in the sky.

A selection of coloured and special effect filters. Clockwise, from the top, there are multi-image, blue, polarising, starburst and red filters.

SPECIAL EFFECTS FILTERS

These can be great fun, but many a picture has been ruined, too! To see how they completely alter your pictures, try experimenting with them on a roll of film first before committing yourself seriously.

Starburst. This produces distinctive highlight points, especially when used at small apertures and on well-lit subjects.

Multi-image. Repeat a favourite image many times in the same picture - or produce a surreal effect!

Diffusing. Also known as a fog or mist filter, this has a clear central spot but a diffused surround which softens detail and reduces contrast.

Speed. This gives the impression of speed by blurring part of the subject, even when stationary!

ACCESSORIES

The number of accessories on the market can be very confusing, because the range is so wide. These pages aim to show some of the more useful ones for the amateur photographer. Think carefully before you buy, and make sure the item is worth the expense.

LENS HOOD

This is to cut out any light which is not needed for the shot. Some lenses have built-in lens hoods, but most are additional clip-on varieties.

CAMERA BAG

A specially designed bag to carry all your camera equipment. There are many makes, shapes, sizes and prices. When choosing one, look for the amount of protection it offers, and size, as well as comfort and convenience for carrying.

TRIPOD

A tripod is sometimes used as a camera support. It allows the camera to be held securely, and stops camera shake or other movement. It is absolutely essential for low-light photography when slow shutter speeds have to be used. Also, if you are using a large telephoto lens, a tripod will take the weight of the camera and lens off your hands and ensure a shake-free result. Look for one that is sturdy but not too heavy, and extends to your height - and higher, as you grow!

NOTEPAD

It is a good idea to keep a note of the photographs you take, including the date, place, aperture and exposure.

LENS BRUSH

It is really important always to keep your lenses and camera clean. Dust always finds a way of getting in. Lens brushes, lens cloths and tissues are designed to remove dust and grit without scratching the lens surface.

CAMERA STRAP

A strap is an inexpensive extra which could save your camera from serious accidental damage.

BATTERIES

Cameras are becoming increasingly dependent upon batteries to power them. Your flash gun needs them, too. Remember what type of batteries your equipment takes and always carry extra batteries with you so you never miss that special picture.

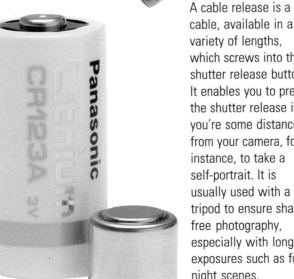

CABLE RELEASE

A cable release is a short cable, available in a variety of lengths, which screws into the shutter release button. It enables you to press the shutter release if you're some distance from your camera, for instance, to take a self-portrait. It is usually used with a tripod to ensure shake-free photography, especially with long exposures such as for night scenes.

41

LANDSCAPES

Many people think a landscape is the easiest thing to photograph, but a beautiful piece of scenery does not always have the same impact on film as it does when first seen. Remember, a photo is a two-dimensional image, so conveying the depth and scale of what you see on to film is important.

DEFINE THE LANDSCAPE

There are many visual elements combining to create a typical landscape. Before you shoot, look hard and think what it is that makes you want to take a photo. Is it the golden cloud patterns in a sunset sky? The water rushing over rocks in a stream? Or a red barn rising above a yellow field of rape? Your lens choice, composition, viewpoint and use of lighting should all be thought about so that you get an accurate record of the scene.

LIGHTING

Early morning and late afternoon are the best times of day for landscape photography. The warm, even glow of this light enhances natural colours and texture. Midday sun should be avoided - on a hot clear day it makes colours look washed-out. A cloudless blue sky should be avoided, too - it can overwhelm a scene.

Early morning: notice the long shadows and highlights.

Late afternoon: notice the intense colour and contrasts.

The interesting shapes of the massed clouds (left) are made more effective by the contrast with the rich yellows of the fields below them.

It might be tempting to include more of the waterfall (below left), but this close-up shot enables you to see the detail of the rocks and water, against the intense green of the moss.

The swathes of colour of these fields (below) are in sharp contrast to the sky, while the curving lines are reflected in the wisps of cloud above.

42

LANDSCAPES

COMPOSITION

Composition is critically important to landscape photography. Make sure you have a focal point, or an object within the scene which gives you an idea of the size and scale of the view. Take your time when looking for exactly the right place from which to take your picture.

Whilst the sunset is what gives the photograph below its attractive tones, it needs a focal point. The fishing boat in the foreground, half in shadow, but highlighted by the reflections on the woodwork, provides this.Try covering up the bottom half of the picture with a piece of paper, and see what a difference it makes.

LENS CHOICE

Wide-angle lenses have good depth of field so it makes sense to feature a foreground subject that's boldly-coloured or -shaped to lead the eye into the picture. Telephoto lenses are best used to draw in close to details and patterns in the landscape which may be too far away physically to move to.

SUNSETS

Probably the most photographed landscape scenes feature a sunset - but they can look a bit bland. For the most striking results, include another subject, such as a fishing boat sailing out to the horizon, to add another point of interest to the picture.

THE FOUR SEASONS

The same landscape setting can look quite different at various times of the year. For instance, the four seasons are best illustrated by taking a photograph of the same piece of scenery from the identical viewpoint at spring, summer, autumn and winter.

There may be an area of countryside or parkland that you visit frequently, which could enable you to do this. Visit it with your camera in the middle of each of the four seasons and take a picture each time. Remember to take your photo from the same spot.

When you study the prints, you'll see how the landscape can vary so much during the course of a year - from the new growth on trees and the flowering of daffodils, crocuses and tulips during spring, to the cold grey light of winter when trees are bare, fields ploughed up, ponds and lakes frozen, and the world transformed. A covering of snow can change the landscape into something special for the camera.

The varying light and colours of the changing seasons can make a familiar scene interesting, as in these pictures of the same oak tree taken at different times of the year. In spring, the branches of the trees are bare but the new growth of winter wheat is showing through; in summer, the tree is surrounded by ripe golden wheat and in autumn, by the paler gold of the stubble; and even on a misty winter's day, it looks stark and dramatic against the snow.

JOINERS

What do you do when the scene you want to shoot is too big for one picture on your camera, and you can't change lenses? A simple and fun answer is to take a series of pictures of different parts of the scene - without moving from your position - in order to join up the picture later. This type of montage is known as a 'joiner'.

When you get the prints back, you can make up the whole scene by joining the prints. They won't match up perfectly, but this is part of the special effect. Try sticking your joiner on a sheet of card and then frame it.

FOREGROUND

Many people make the mistake of not paying enough attention to the foreground in a landscape photograph. This is easily done, as your attention is usually drawn to some beautiful scenery or buildings in the distance.

A landscape can be much improved by including some foreground interest to add colour as well as scale to the composition. Often the best scenes are those which include people or animals in the foreground.

PANORAMA

Landscapes and skylines are perfect subjects for panorama pictures. These are long horizontal photographs which emphasize spectacular horizons such as mountain ranges or city skylines. Kodak, Fuji and Konica make cheap, disposable panorama cameras already loaded with film for up to 24 pictures in this format. When you have finished your film, take the camera to your chemist or high street processing lab and tell them that these are panorama pictures. They will take the film, process it and make up the specially long panorama prints.

SPORTS PHOTOGRAPHY

GET CLOSE TO THE ACTION

When you watch tennis, football or test cricket on TV you may have noticed that all the photographers use long telephoto lenses. These allow them to home in on the action without getting too close to it. These are specialist lenses, but the lesson can be applied to your own photography: a typical telephoto zoom lens will give you all the flexibility you'll need for framing action photos; or you may physically need to move closer if you are using a compact camera.

Before the game, match or race begins, make sure you are in the best possible position to take your action shots. Try to wait until the activity is at its height; when a goal is scored, a point is won, or something exciting happens.

Unlike landscape photography, where you can take your time to set up your composition, shooting sports pictures requires quick decisions and fast reactions. For this reason it may seem difficult to master, but the techniques are few. It just takes time and practice and lots of film to become good at it. The secret is a good position, patience, and a tripod to support a long lens.

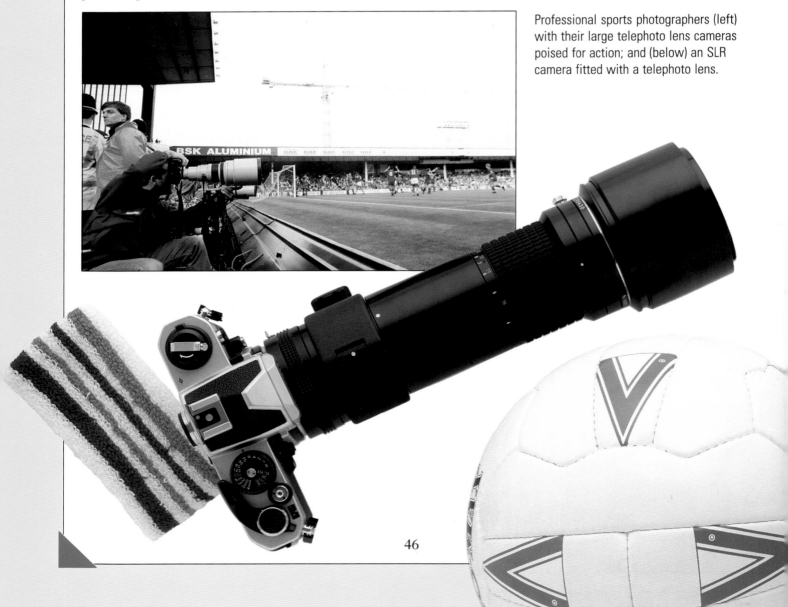

Professional sports photographers (left) with their large telephoto lens cameras poised for action; and (below) an SLR camera fitted with a telephoto lens.

46

SPORTS PHOTOGRAPHY

SHUTTER SPEEDS

For such sports as football and tennis 1/500sec is probably the slowest shutter speed you should use. Image blur will appear on slower speeds. Faster-moving subjects require faster shutter speeds to stop the action. Alternatively, a very slow shutter speed, say 1/sec, gives an impression of soft movement, so long as the subject is kept in frame during the exposure and the camera is held steady.

PANNING

This involves the photographer following the subject with his camera as it moves across in front of him. The result is a sharp subject against a blurred background. Fast film can help achieve this effect.

READY AND WAITING

This is a technique devised for getting sharp shots of fast-moving subjects heading straight for the camera. All you have to do is focus your lens on a point in the frame, such as the brow of a hill or a curve in the track, where you know the subject will appear. When the car or bike or horse enters this zone, press the shutter button. Don't hesitate, or the shot will be lost.

A good example (below) of a panning shot: the camera was ready and focused, then followed the biker as he moved.

ACTION SEQUENCES

Motordrives are either built-in or optional extras to most SLR cameras. With them you can take a picture sequence which records dramatic changes in a sport by taking shots continuously as long as you press the shutter button. Be warned, it uses film up fast!

TELLING A STORY

Every weekend of the year there is a sports match taking place at a local playing field somewhere near you: football, hockey, tennis, cricket, rugby, baseball, or athletics. Any one of these can provide a good sequence of pictures.

The key is to watch the sport beforehand to find out where most of the play takes place, and the peaks of the action.

PHOTOGRAPHING TENNIS

Tennis can be more easily photographed because the action moves from one end of the court to the other at a fairly constant pace.

You could stand on a bench or box behind the baseline, pointing your camera at the player on the other side of the net. Don't take her picture until she is just about to hit the ball, as this is the point when the action is slowest.

Move to the edge of the baseline, and turn your camera upright to take a picture of the player about to serve. The best time to press the shutter release is when the ball has been tossed up in the air, as this is the instant when the player is poised and relatively still before completing the serve.

From the side of the court, near the net, you are in a good position to alternate from one player to the other, but don't take your picture until a player has swung their arm back ready to hit the ball - the best sports action shots always have the ball in the frame.

When the match is over, save a few frames for the winning player, who might shout and cheer, or throw his or her arms up in the air.

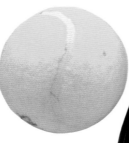

Capturing the moment of tension: the player is poised ready to hit the ball.

By focusing on the other player and waiting, the photographer has caught the moment of impact of the ball on the racquet.

The winner triumphant: save a few exposures for the last minutes of the game.

SPORTING PEAKS

Some of the best sports pictures are taken when the action is at its slowest: for example, when a pole vaulter has reached the bar, he has in fact stopped moving before falling down; or when any ball reaches its highest point, it stops for a split second before descending.

The finishing line of a sprint race: you can sense the movement of the runners, as they approach the tape.

Swimmers diving from the starting blocks.

A baseball pitcher at full stretch, just about to release the ball.

A pole vaulter who has just cleared the bar.

In many sports, there are set plays which enable you to compose and focus your camera on the peak of the action.

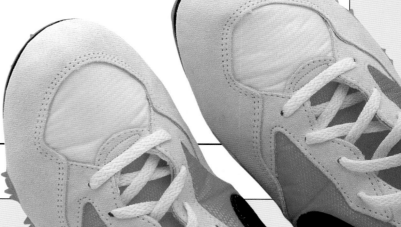

NATURE PHOTOGRAPHY

The secret to successful nature photography is observation. Go out into your back garden and see what is happening on a typical spring or summer's day. It shouldn't take long for you to see a wide range of subjects to photograph.

FLOWERS
There is hardly a colour on earth that cannot be found on the petals of a flower. Roses, tulips, daffodils, geraniums and violets are all richly coloured. Or you may find that delicate, pale flowers against a dark background can make a striking photograph. You can take flower pictures indoors or outdoors, from different angles - at the level of the flowers, or from above, looking down - or simply arrange a vase of flowers and capture its beauty.

An interesting view of a field of sunflowers: taken from above, looking down.

A change of angle gives a quite different effect: the flowers are more 'face on', with a dark skyline lowering behind them.

Nuts on a bird table in winter will attract lots of birds for you to photograph. You'll have to be very patient and keep still, so you need to be in position before the birds arrive.

BIRDS
Birds may seem difficult subjects to photograph, but there are some simple ways of capturing them on film. Birds have favourite perches - a branch, a fence, the eaves of a roof - so when you have spotted such a perch, focus on this position. Keep very quiet and still, because birds are easily startled. When the bird perches, take the picture. This same approach can be used to even greater effect if you have a bird feeding table, as it can be the most fascinating focus for wildlife.

BIRD TABLES
The winter months are among the best for bird photography, as food is in short supply in the wild. This enables you to coax birds to your back garden by placing seed, nuts and other food on a table. Bird feeding tables are sold in most garden centres, but any piece of outdoor furniture will do, even a tree stump. This will then give you an obvious aspect to focus on and compose your picture.

HIDES AND COVER

Birds, squirrels and other wild animals are very wary of people, so it is important to stay hidden and quiet.

A garden shed can be a good hide if it has a knot hole in the wood, or a window with a curtain, through which you can point your camera. There is a slight risk of reflection and flare off the glass, however. If you live near a wildlife reserve, there may be special bird hides with openings suitable for your camera.

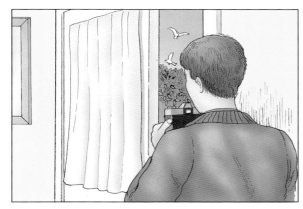

Another good position would be from a back door or french window - open the door, draw the curtains, and point the camera between the curtains. As nature photography requires a lot of patience and waiting, it makes sense to have your camera resting on a table, or on a tripod, to keep it still and in the right position.

This ocelot (right) is well behind the wire mesh of its enclosure. If you focus on its eyes and use a wide aperture, the mesh in the foreground goes out of focus and disappears.

AT THE ZOO

All zoos welcome photography, but you should always observe the safety signs and barriers.

Bars, wire mesh or glass form the main barriers between you and the animals, and will usually be seen on your photos.

With an SLR camera, focus in on the eyes of your subject, and the viewfinder will show the mesh as blurred: the more you turn the aperture ring, the further it will defocus. This technique can be applied to bars too, but they are too thick to disappear totally, and will still form an impression.

Aquariums and reptile houses all use glass as a barrier. To reduce the chance of reflections, rest the edge of your lens gently on the surface of the glass. Cup your hand around the outside of the lens, and do not use flash.

PHOTO HINT
When shooting close-ups of flowers or small animals be careful not to cast your own shadow over the subject, otherwise the photograph will be dull.

PETS

Cats, dogs and other domestic animals are obvious subjects to photograph because they are used to your presence, and will usually let you get as close as you want with your camera. Be prepared, and you may get some unusual or interesting shots.

GREEN-EYE!

It's best to avoid direct flash when taking close-up pictures of animals. This is because direct flash causes a similar effect to red-eye in people. With cats, direct flash causes their eyes to appear green in colour photos.

All pets have favourite places to sleep, especially cats, so watch where your pet likes to go and next time be prepared with your camera to capture that moment when it is most relaxed. You may come up with some surprising photos!

Cats have very striking eyes, so take a close-up, focusing on the eyes and filling the whole frame with the head of the cat. This type of shot will emphasize the power of the cat's eyes.

Kittens and puppies are full of energy and very playful. The bundle of wool, the rubber bone and the tennis ball are useful props to help you photograph your pet at play.

FISH TANKS

Goldfish bowls and fish tanks present a different set of problems for the photographer.

Goldfish bowls cause a lot of distortion, because the curve makes the fish look bigger than it really is. Get as close as you can to focus, and wait for the fish to swim into view near the glass. A flat-sided glass tank causes far less distortion.

Many tanks feature an overhead fluorescent light which illuminates the water very well. The only problem is that fluorescent light causes a green cast to register on film. This can be avoided by placing a special filter on the end of your camera lens.

It is said that owners often grow to look like their pets. If you think it's true, take some pictures of the owner with their pet, face to face or side by side.

OUTDOORS

The greenery and extra space of the garden, with bright, even outdoor light, is usually a better location for photographing dogs, because they aren't as comfortable within the confines of a house as cats. Outside, you and your subject will have more freedom of movement. If a dog has a kennel, take a picture of it looking out of the kennel.

These puppies feel safe and at ease because they're 'at home'! Pets are easiest to photograph when they're contented.

STILL LIFE

AT HOME

Still life is one subject you can easily do at home. A suitable working area would be a table or bench near a window. Window lighting, especially the even light you get from an overcast day, will give enough light to emphasize the line, shape and texture of your subject. Or household lightbulbs (tungsten lamps) produce a warm, orange type of light on normal daylight film, which suits many still life scenes.

The subject of your still life could be either one or a group of everyday objects such as a vase, eggs, a bottle, glasses, even a loaf of bread. If you're using a group of similar objects like fruit or flowers, try different arrangements to see how the lighting falls on each, and which overall shape looks the best.

You can achieve dramatic results by using coloured lights and shooting your still life from different angles, even from above.

Still life photography captures on film the everyday objects around us. The secret of still life is simplicity - of subject, composition and lighting. Your camera set-up should be simple, too. The advantage of still life is that you can control every aspect of it, so use your time to design and compose the subject and arrange the lighting carefully. You can use familiar objects easily available around the house, or make up extraordinary combinations just for fun. Or pick a theme, such as sports or food, for your collection of objects.

BACKGROUNDS

A background should help emphasize the focal point of any composition, particularly still life. Choose a white or neutral-coloured wall, or use a piece of clean white card to emphasize shape and line. Alternatively, black backgrounds hide shadows and give contrast to highlights.

REFLECTORS

Gold and silver reflectors are used to reflect window light, to fill in shadows. Kitchen foil stretched across a large piece of card is a good cheap way of making a reflector. A large piece of white card or paper, or even newspaper, can reflect the sunlight to illuminate shadow detail in some still life studies.

KEEP IT STEADY

To get a perfect still life photo, the camera must be very steady. Support it on a table, bean bag, box, or any other available surface, to make sure that it does not shake as you take the picture. If you have them, a tripod and cable release could be used for a completely shake-free result.

Your still life arrangement won't move, but your hand might - so using a tripod is the safest way to avoid camera-shake.

PEOPLE

When you take a picture of someone, try to capture something about that person's life or personality in your photograph. Whether it is an important occasion like a wedding, or a shot of someone on holiday, your photo should try to convey something more of that person than merely what they look like. Remember that every picture tells a story.

GROUP SHOTS

The problem with group shots is that the more people you have, the greater the chance of someone suddenly moving, blinking, or looking away from the camera when you press the shutter button. Keep everyone relaxed and don't ask them to look at the camera until you're definitely ready to focus your picture. If you ask them to smile, don't keep them waiting - they won't like it and their smiles will look strained by the time you release the shutter. Get them in position first, compose your picture and focus - *then* tell everyone to say 'cheese'.

CANDIDS

When a subject doesn't know they are being photographed, it is called a candid shot. These can be the most satisfying pictures of people because you never know whom you're going to see and photograph next. Capture the face as well as the surrounding environment for a more dramatic result.

When young children are involved and interested in something, like this rabbit, they are at their most natural and you will get the most effective candid photographs.

If you stand near the official photographer, but to one side, your photos may be more natural, as people are not looking directly at you. For wedding photographs, *always* focus on the bride.

FAMILY TREE

There are probably three generations in your immediate family, as well as aunts, uncles, cousins, nieces and nephews, who all form a part of your family tree. Your mum and dad could help you draw the tree with the right birth dates and connections, and then you can go about photographing every member of your family. You may be surprised to find out how big your family is!

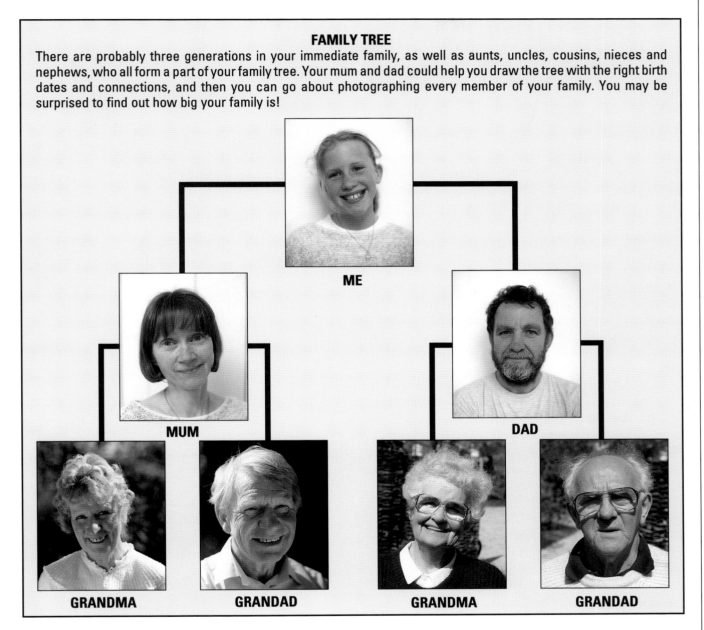

ME

MUM

DAD

GRANDMA

GRANDAD

GRANDMA

GRANDAD

NEWS PICTURES

The photographs which stay in our memories the longest are usually pictures of people we know. It is no surprise, therefore, that the more a person's picture is published and seen, the more famous that person - and that picture - becomes.

Newspaper photographers always try to get a different picture, no matter how many times they have photographed someone. Here is a list of a few things you can change in order to get an original photo of the same person every time:

1. Pick a different location or background.
2. Try a low angle, with them looking down on you.
3. Ask them to wear a hat.
4. If they wear glasses, tell them to take them off.
5. With the sun behind your subject, use flash.
6. Ask them to dress up in unusual clothes.

PORTRAITS

A portrait is a formal photograph of someone posing for the camera. Most portraits are taken with the camera upturned, because it gives better framing for head and shoulder compositions, as well as full length studies.

SET-UP AND LIGHTING
Set up your camera in your chosen position ready for shooting. Keep your lighting set-up simple by having your model sit near a window. A reflector placed on the other side of your sitter should be positioned to reflect the light from the window on to the 'shadow side' of their face.

Don't ask your model to sit down until you know exactly how you want them to pose and are ready to take pictures. It's better for them to sit because they will be more comfortable and relaxed. You could then vary the position you shoot from, and try some photos with flash on your camera as well. Remember to keep your camera at eye level with your sitter.

MOOD AND SURROUNDINGS
The room where you shoot should be cleared in advance of anything you don't want included in the frame - your background should be uncluttered. Play some music to relax your model, and establish the mood you want to create.

Talk to your model about the way you want them to look for the camera. Take lots of pictures, changing the pose and expression of your model frequently - both of you will feel more confident and relaxed as the session develops.

Have your model looking out of the window for a pensive study, or looking just past the camera at something in the distance. Tell a few stories and jokes, and watch your model's changing expressions, taking pictures as their mood changes.

Make sure your model is feeling relaxed and comfortable before you start to take your photographs.

You could talk, tell her a few stories or even ask her to show you different facial expressions.

Be prepared to take a number of shots, and you'll be able to show her looking cheerful, thoughtful, angry...

... or even amazed!

CHILDREN AND BABIES

The most important thing to remember about photographing children and babies is to get down to their level so that your camera is not at a strange angle. This will make your pictures look more natural. Keep them occupied with toys, and don't try to interrupt their play!

SELF PORTRAITS

Using the same set-up as for normal portraits, put something in the chair you will be sitting in to focus on. Activate the self-timer on your camera, then press the shutter button and take up your position for the camera. Self-timers have a 10-second shutter release delay, and may have a flashing red light on the front of the camera or audible beeping to let you know it's about to shoot.

If your camera does not have a self-timer, you could take a photo of yourself in a mirror - an action shot of the photographer at work!

You could take a photograph of yourself in the mirror, or even ask someone else to take a photo of you in the mirror!

HANDY HINTS
If your model's hands are to be included in the portrait, it is important to position them well for the camera. The simplest way is for your model to clasp his/her hands in their lap.

HOLIDAY SNAPS

Holidays are the best time for taking pictures. The time is yours, you're feeling relaxed and happy, the weather is often good and there are plenty of new places, locations and people to photograph. It's not surprising, then, that many people take their best photographs on holiday.

BE READY!

The ideal camera to take on holiday is one that you can take anywhere with ease. It should be small, easy to use and light to carry, enabling you to point and shoot wherever you are. There are many top quality auto focus compact cameras on the market today which have a built-in flash and zoom lens. Some are also weatherproof, which means you can take them to the beach and not worry about sand and water affecting performance.

WHEN TO SHOOT

In hot climates or on beach resorts, it's not a good idea to take pictures when the sun is high. It is usually too glary, colours become bleached and shadows are harsh. On a beach, or anywhere near water, there is a lot of reflected light as well as the direct light of the sun, so it is best when outdoors to shoot either in the morning or late afternoon when the sun is lower in the sky. (If you go on a skiing holiday, the same thing applies: the snow will reflect the light as much as sand and water.)

If your camera has a built-in flash, remember to use it if you're photographing someone with the light behind them, otherwise the camera will expose for the brightness of the background, and your subject will come out as a silhouette.

There could have been a lot of glare in this holiday scene, with the white sand and sea, both of which will reflect the bright light. But the long shadows are the key: the late afternoon sun was not too dazzling, and the angle the photo was taken from avoids reflections from the surface of the water. The children are absorbed in their activities, so look totally natural and happy.

SUNBURN

It's not just people that can suffer from too much sun - cameras, too, should not be left lying in the sun or on hot sand. If you are spending a lot of time sunbathing, keep your camera in a cool spot, in the shade or in a bag when not in use. Weatherproof cameras may be sand and water resistant, but they should be treated with care and not immersed in water - they are not underwater cameras.

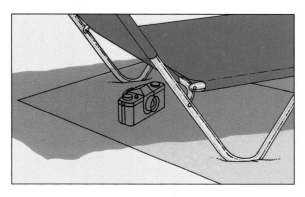

People are usually happy to be photographed in the warmth and sunshine of a holiday atmosphere - or you might even catch them relaxing unawares!

PEOPLE

People are much more relaxed and happier about being photographed on holiday than when at home, so use this time as an opportunity to get some original people pictures. Photograph them asleep in the sun, licking an ice cream, diving into a swimming pool, reading a book, or dancing at a pool party in the evening.

THE PHOTO STORY

Every picture tells a story, so the saying goes. Why not take that one stage further by telling a larger story with a sequence of photos? Photo stories can be created in just a handful of shots. The trick is to pick the occasion first and plan the story and pictures you want to take in advance.

PICKING THE OCCASION

Your brother's birthday, your parents' wedding anniversary, a family wedding, Christmas, New Year's Eve, Hallowe'en - these are some of the events that could form the basis of a photo story, and they all happen on the same date every year, making it easier for you to plan ahead.

Photo stories in magazines use photographs to tell a story: why not use the idea, and make up your own photo story?

WRITING THE STORYLINE

If your photo story is to comprise, say, six photos, what should they be made up of? You could look at some photo story magazines or comics for ideas. You could write a mystery, love or ghost story, and then persuade your family and friends - even your pets - to take part and be the subjects for your pictures.

STORYBOARD

Writers of TV shows, movies and videos draw out storyboards which are rough sketches of each scene. They show the sequence of the story to be shot. By doing the same thing for your photo story, you can have a visual description of the photos you want to take and the order they are to run. The storyboard will also help everyone who is to feature in your pictures understand what their role is and what the story is about.

THE PHOTO STORY

THE SEQUENCE

Choose a situation that you are familiar with, and see if you can work out a sequence of events which tell a story. It could be a family gathering, or a day in the life of your pet - or you could make up your own mystery, ghost or love story! Here is a suggested sequence of six pictures to tell a story about the joys of being in the garden on a summer's day.

1. Right - here goes, then. I suppose I'd better get to work.

2. Better just check that it's got some petrol in.

3. Here I am, slaving away on a boiling hot day ...

4. What do you think of that for a professional job, eh?

5. This is the bit the public don't see. But it's all good compost ...

6. And now - for a well-deserved rest!

MOUNTING AND DISPLAY

A good photograph deserves to be displayed. Whether in a photo album or mounted in a frame, each picture can be a special reminder of an event, a person or a favourite pet. A well-displayed picture makes an impression on everyone who sees it.

THE PHOTO ALBUM

Albums are convenient to handle, and many photographs can be displayed at one time. Think carefully about how you want to plan your album. Do you want to follow a logical sequence of events, such as what happened on holiday, or perhaps have a whole album of pictures of your pet, or your family?

You may like to add captions, either written directly on to the pages, or typed on sticky labels. These can add a whole new dimension to your photographs.

BEYOND THE PHOTO ALBUM

You may want to enlarge and frame a favourite picture. Many picture framers are now geared to mounting photographs as well as paintings. They offer a variety of frames and borders which complement the colours and tones of your print. It can be expensive, but there is a cheaper alternative for a similar high quality result - do it yourself!

There is a wide range of picture frames, mounts and albums that you can buy, from the inexpensive to the much more expensive ones - for your very special photograph, or for a gift.

PHOTO HINT
Use card that is at least one size up from the dimensions of your print - eg: if your print is 25 x 20cm, use card that is 30 x 25cm as your border.

DISPLAYING YOUR PHOTOS

Think carefully about the best place to display your photos. You may want to cover your bedroom walls with photos, or perhaps take some to school to decorate your desk or locker. Perhaps a well-framed picture would look good in a main room in your house, or a diary or address book with your photos on the front would make an unusual gift.

A collection of your best photographs, enlarged and framed, makes a bright and cheerful display on the wall.

MOUNTING A PRINT

1. Using a ruler and pencil, measure the area of the print that is to be seen when mounted and mark these border lines on the print.

2. Mark these border dimensions on the back of a sheet of thick card. Use a craft knife or angled cutter (this and the mounting card can be bought from an artist's supply shop) to cut along these border lines to make your frame.

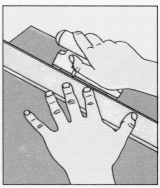

3. On a second sheet of card (the same dimensions as the first), place the print centrally and glue into place. This is the backing card. Use tracing paper over the print to protect it from marks.

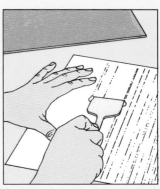

4. Now apply glue or adhesive to the edges of the backing card, being careful not to get any on the print.

5. Carefully position the top piece of card down on to the backing card and press firmly, making sure the edges of each card match. Once dry, it is now ready for display.

65

COLOUR SLIDES

Also known as colour reversal or transparencies, colour slides are popular because the colours are truer to life than prints, and you can use them to put on an exciting slide show for your friends and family.

PROCESS PAID
Most slide films are sold at a price which includes the cost of processing. The film box contains an envelope which you use to post your exposed film to the processsing laboratory. Your processed slides will arrive back by post in a box, individually mounted and numbered.

STORING YOUR SLIDES
The box and slide mounts are very useful when caring for and storing your slides. You can use the mount to stick down a small adhesive label with relevant information about the picture: what it is, where it was taken and when.

THE SLIDE PROJECTOR
A slide projector should be used for your slide show. Your room must be dark, and a white wall could serve as a screen. The projector should be placed on a flat, level table, about 1-3m from the wall for the best results.

PLASTIC SLIDE SLEEVES

Plastic slide sleeves are a good means of storage and allow you quick reference to a large number of pictures without you having to handle them one at a time. These can be kept in a ring binder or fitted into a filing cabinet.

THE SLIDE SHOW

This can be a dreaded part of photography. In fact, done properly, and with imagination, it can be fun. Seeing your photographs projected onto a screen is very exciting, especially if you are showing them to a group of people who like what they see.

When putting together a slide show, remember you are telling a story in pictures. Do not use too many slides. Peoples' attention spans are brief - rarely more than 20 minutes - so set a time limit for your slide show. Don't keep a slide up for too long, and keep the sequence moving at a brisk pace.

The best place to start a story is at the beginning. For example, if your show is to be of a recent holiday abroad, then start at the preparation - pictures of the packing, then move your sequence on in the order that things happened: the airport, the flight, arrival, hotel, trips to the beach, sightseeing, shopping, meals, evenings out, homeward bound.

Interesting sequences can be put together within the slide show, such as shots of local people or fellow travellers, local architecture, similar colours or shapes.

Above all, keep it simple. As a finishing touch, try adding music. Music is much more relaxing to listen to than a commentary on every slide.

CARING FOR YOUR SLIDES

To keep your slides dust free, use a clean, dry, anti-static lens cleaner, or use a blower brush.

THE PROFESSIONALS

Professional photographers use a darkroom to process their films and make prints. A darkroom, as the name suggests, is a room which is totally blocked off from any light source, except a safelight (a dim, orange light source which won't damage films and paper).

BLACK AND WHITE

Black and white film processing is the simplest of the film processes in terms of the chemicals you need and the temperature at which these chemicals have to be used.

DEVELOPING BLACK AND WHITE FILM

1. Film from the camera is loaded, in complete darkness, onto a spiral plastic reel.

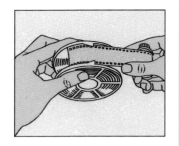

2. The reel fits into a developing tank and the lid is screwed on. This has a special light-proof hole through which the developing solutions can be poured.

3. Three main chemicals, warmed to 20°C, are used to make the image permanent and ready to be printed. These chemicals are developer, stop bath and fixer.

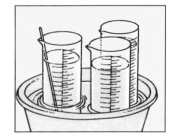

4. Each is poured in turn into the tank, which is then shaken well so that the film is thoroughly exposed to it, and then poured away.

5. Cold running water is used to wash off all traces of the chemicals.

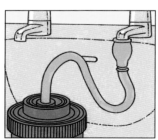

6. The film (or 'negative') is then hung up to dry.

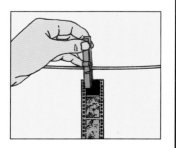

PRINTING BLACK AND WHITE FILM

1. The negative is placed in the negative carrier of the enlarger. An orange 'safelight' will need to be used, as photographic paper is sensitive to white light.

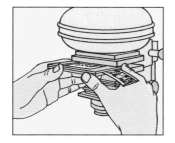

2. The size and focus of the print is checked on plain paper, then photographic paper is placed on the base-board and exposed to the light from the en-larger.

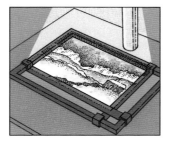

3. The print is placed in print developer at a temperature of 20°C, and moved about gently.

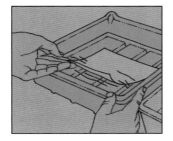

4. Gradually the image begins to appear. When it has been developed for long enough, the print is placed in stop bath (to stop it developing any more) and then fixer.

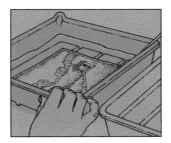

5. The print needs to be washed under running water for about half an hour to rinse off the chemicals.

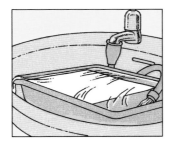

6. The print (or 'positive') is then hung up to dry.

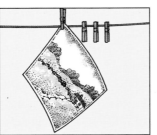

COLOUR

Developing and printing colour starts in the same way as black and white, as the film is loaded into a spiral and the three chemicals are added one at a time, being washed off after each one has been used.

When printing colour film, it is important to get the balance of colours right. Mixtures of magenta (red), yellow and cyan (blue) are used in this process. The correct balance will leave you with a bright picture which is as true to life as possible. The wrong balance, however, can lead to all sorts of strange colours, and may spoil an otherwise perfect picture.

CONTACT PRINTS

A professional may try making contact prints to make sure the photo prints correctly. He may expose a negative three times, for 4, 8 and 16 seconds. In a well-lit room they can be compared to make sure he is happy with the results achieved. Going through this process can make it clear whether the paper chosen is too low or high a grade for the desired image. It can also show whether the prints are too dark, meaning that the exposure time should be reduced, or too light, meaning that the exposure time should be increased.

A set of 'contact' prints - printed directly from the film negative on to photographic paper.

COMMON PROBLEMS

Sometimes your prints may look too pink or yellow. It could be that the colour filtration at the processor was not correctly balanced. If your negatives are undamaged, you can have a new set of prints made.

There may be flashes of white or colours at the edge of your print. This is probably caused by light getting in to the back of your camera. Always check that the back is firmly closed after you have loaded a film.

If your print is very blurred, it may be that you did not hold the camera steady enough when you took the photograph. Re-read the tips on pages 14-15 about camera shake.

If one part of the print is blurred, it could be that there was a drop of moisture on the lens. Be careful when in the snow or near water to keep your lens dry.

Shiny-looking white patches on a print can be caused by light from the flash being reflected back from glossy or reflective surfaces, such as mirrors or glass.

If your print has a white line across it, check on the negative: this may be scratched. Make sure that the inside of your camera is free of grit and dust.

SPECIAL EFFECTS

Effects can be created by a professional which could make your prints look very special. One technique they may use is called 'burning'.

This involves taking a piece of card large enough to cover the printing area, and cutting out holes corresponding to the areas you want to emphasize, or 'burn in'.

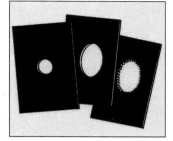

When most of the print has been exposed, it is covered with the card, so that only certain areas receive light. If the card is kept moving, a shadowy area forms around the edge, making it look like an antique picture. This *vignette* effect works particularly well with portraits.

PROTECTING NEGATIVES

When your pictures are returned after being processed, make sure you keep the negatives in their protective wallet. Then if you want to make any further prints in the future, the negatives will be in the perfect condition to do so. Always keep them free of water, dust and dirt, and in a safe place.

THE FUTURE?

In time, you may want to develop your photography so that you are able to process and print your own photos. It is exciting to have complete control of such an interesting and involving hobby, and can give you extra hours of fun. But be warned, it is hard work too!

In a photographic lab, your favourite pictures can be turned into all sorts of other things - table mats, posters, postcards, and a pretend oil painting! These are good gift ideas, and can make a real feature of that special photo.

COMPETITIONS

Photographic competitions are a good means of getting your photographs seen and, if successful, rewarded. There are dozens of photographic competitions going on at any one time, organized by photo magazines such as *Amateur Photographer* or major camera and film manufacturers such as Canon, Olympus, Kodak and Fuji.

READ THE RULES

Always read the rules, including the fine print. Some people are disqualified because their entry breaks one of the rules. Rules give details and conditions about who can enter, the quantity, size and format of photos acceptable, the closing date for entries and other information about the judging and organization of the competition.

GOLDEN RULES

Always send a stamped self-addressed envelope for the return of your entry.

If your entry is a slide, never send it in a glass mount. No matter how much padded packaging you use, the glass will always break and scratch the film.

Don't send mounted prints. These too can be damaged in the post.

Only enter competitions that say 'copyright remains with the photographer'. Unfortunately, some competition organizers have rules which give them copyright ownership over all photos entered. It means that the company could keep your photo and use it without paying you a fee.

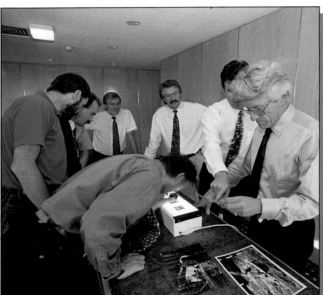

The judges look very carefully at all the photographs submitted in a competition. Make sure that you follow the rules, and your entry keeps to the theme suggested. One day you may be a prizewinner!

THINK BEFORE YOU SHOOT
In any competition original ideas will always be noticed. How well you carry them out depends on how well you plan and prepare. Good luck!

WHAT JUDGES LOOK FOR

Experienced competition judges look for accurate focusing, imaginative use of light, strong composition and visual impact. If you have kept to the subject theme and rules of the competition, your entry's chances of success will hinge on how far you have reached these standards - and, of course, the quantity and quality of the other entries.

Taking a shot from an unusual angle may give you an advantage in an entry for 'A view of the city'.

This picture looks natural and the two children are obviously having fun: an ideal entry for the theme of 'Happiness'.

'Pets' is a popular subject: here the colour and texture of the tree trunks provide a beautiful background to this cat.

'A landscape' - from the stark tree in the foreground to the hazy horizon, this picture conveys a superb sense of distance.

ADVANCED PHOTOGRAPHY

So where do you go from here? How do you advance and improve your photography once you have achieved a level of understanding and experience of the basics? There are so many branches and applications of photography that trying to master them all would be a mistake, as well as impossible!

A selection of photography magazines from various countries around the world. You can learn a lot, and gain ideas and tips about technique, from reading magazines of this type.

FINDING YOUR STRENGTHS

Think about what you enjoy photographing the most, then look at all your photos and see which type of pictures you do the best. The more pictures you take, the sooner you will discover your strengths and weaknesses. Concentrate on your strengths. If it's landscapes, think about how you can improve them. Getting a tripod would give you a lot more scope. Adding some filters to your kit will also give you more options. If wildlife photography is your favourite, a long telephoto lens may be worth saving up for to allow you to get closer to your elusive subject. Whatever your chosen field, think about what additional pieces of equipment or accessories you need to improve your pictures.

CLUBS AND SOCIETIES

In every major town you are likely to find a local camera club or society. They regularly hold competitions and events which are fun to join in. Talking to fellow amateur photographers and seeing their pictures can give you lots of new ideas.

Photography can be a great hobby - one you may enjoy for the rest of your life. Good luck!

The author's favourite photograph from all those he has taken. If you are keen, you may decide on a career in photography.

INDEX

Italic figures refer to captions or to illustration labels.